THIS BOOK BELONGS TO

....

HELLO FRIENDS!

Welcome to a world of relaxation, creativity, and self-discovery! Our coloring book is a delightful escape into a world of intricate designs and artistic expression.

Within these pages, you'll find intricate designs and patterns designed to captivate your imagination and provide a soothing escape from the demands of daily life.

Each page is a canvas awaiting your personal touch, an opportunity to infuse vibrant hues into beautifully crafted patterns. Immerse yourself in the art of coloring and let the stress melt away.

USEFUL TIP

Our paper is perfect for colored pencils, crayons, pastels, and alcohol-based markers.

To prevent bleed-through, especially with wet mediums, place a blank sheet underneath the page you're coloring.

Tiny Daisy

SHARING, LEARNING AND COLORING TIPS

If you have any questions or concerns please feel free to contact us at support@tinydaisy.com! We're here to assist and ensure your coloring journey is the best ever!

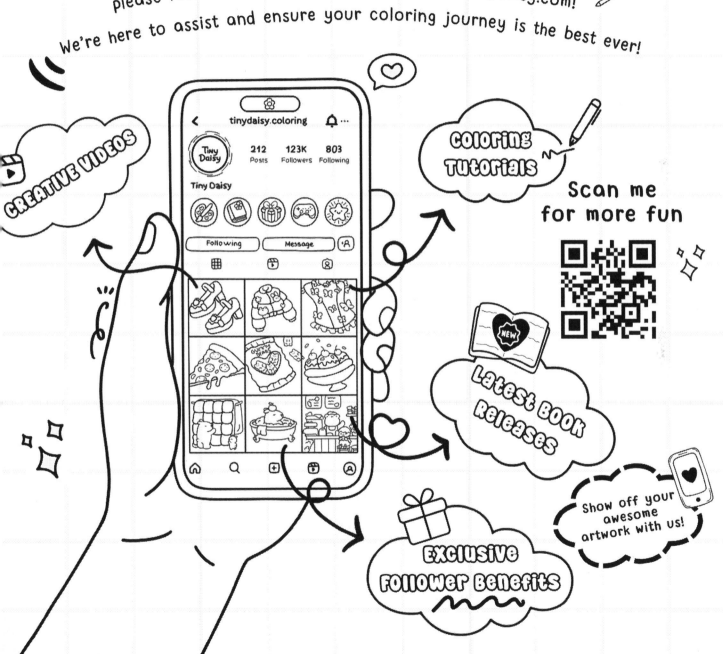

CREATIVE VIDEOS

Coloring Tutorials

Scan me for more fun

Latest Book Releases

Exclusive Follower Benefits

Show off your awesome artwork with us!

COLOR TEST PAGE

Thank You

Dear Beloved Customers,

Thank you for choosing my coloring book. Your support means the world to me, and I hope you enjoyed every moment spent bringing these pages to life with your creativity. As an author and artist, your feedback is invaluable in helping me create even better books for you in the future.

If you enjoyed this book, I would greatly appreciate it if you could leave a 5-star review or write a short review on Amazon.

To make it convenient, I have provided a QR code below. Your review helps other readers discover and enjoy my work, or it helps me improve future products if there was anything that didn't meet your expectations.

Thank you for trusting and becoming my customer. I hope my products will continue to bring joy and creativity to your life.

With heartfelt gratitude,

Sincerely,

TinyDaisy

Made in the USA
Columbia, SC
26 October 2024

45122449R00050